Parisa
the
Pilot
Marcy Schaaf
AF421808

Introduction

Welcome to the inspiring story of Parisa the Pilot! This tale takes you on a journey from a young girl's dreams to the skies she conquers with determination and courage. Parisa, a spirited and ambitious girl from the Middle East, always dreamed of flying high above the clouds. Despite being told that girls can't be pilots, Parisa never gave up on her dream.

Through hard work, perseverance, and an unshakable belief in herself, Parisa not only achieves her dream but also becomes a beacon of inspiration for girls everywhere. This story is a celebration of breaking barriers, overcoming stereotypes, and proving that with dedication, any dream is possible.

Join Parisa on her incredible adventure from dreaming under the stars to soaring through the sky as a skilled pilot. Let her story remind you that no dream is too big and no goal is out of reach. Girls can do anything they set their minds to—including becoming pilots!

Dedication

To Whitney Love,

Your unwavering determination and relentless pursuit of your dream have always been an inspiration to me and everyone around you. Watching you never forget your goal and finally take the brave step to start flight school at age 32 Fills my heart with immense pride.

This book is dedicated to you, Whitney, for reminding us all that dreams have no expiration date and that with hard work and persistence, anything is possible.

With all my love and pride,
Mom

In the Middle East lived a
girl named Parisa.
She had a big dream.

Parisa
dreamed of being a pilot!

But people told Parisa
"Girls can't be pilots."
Parisa didn't believe them.

She knew she could fly if she worked hard and never gave up.

Every night, Parisa would look at the
stars and imagine herself zooming
through the skies.

"I will be a pilot!" she exclaimed, filled with determination.

Years went by but Parisa never forgot her dream of flying.

At age 32, Parisa saw an ad for flight school. "PILOTS NEEDED" it said!

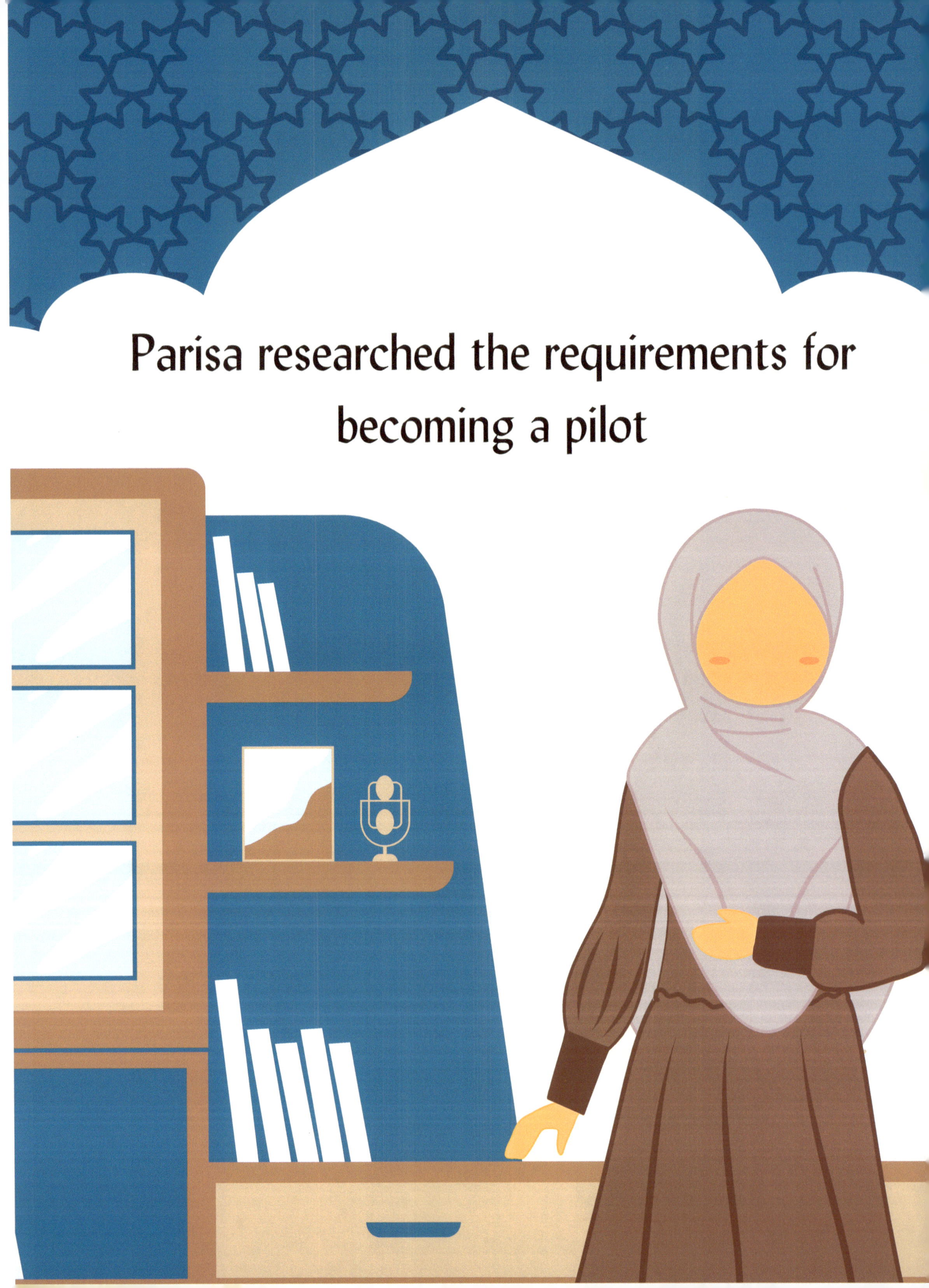

Parisa researched the requirements for becoming a pilot

She applied to flight schools, determined
to follow her dream.

Parisa was accepted into flight school!
She was thrilled.

Parisa learned about maps, control panels, and communicating with the tower.

She practiced flying, ensuring she was
ready for every situation.

Parisa studied weather patterns, safety protocols, and emergency procedures.

She met the tough training requirements, working day and night.

Finally, Parisa graduated from flight school, achieving a major milestone.

It was time for Parisa's first commercial flight with passengers.

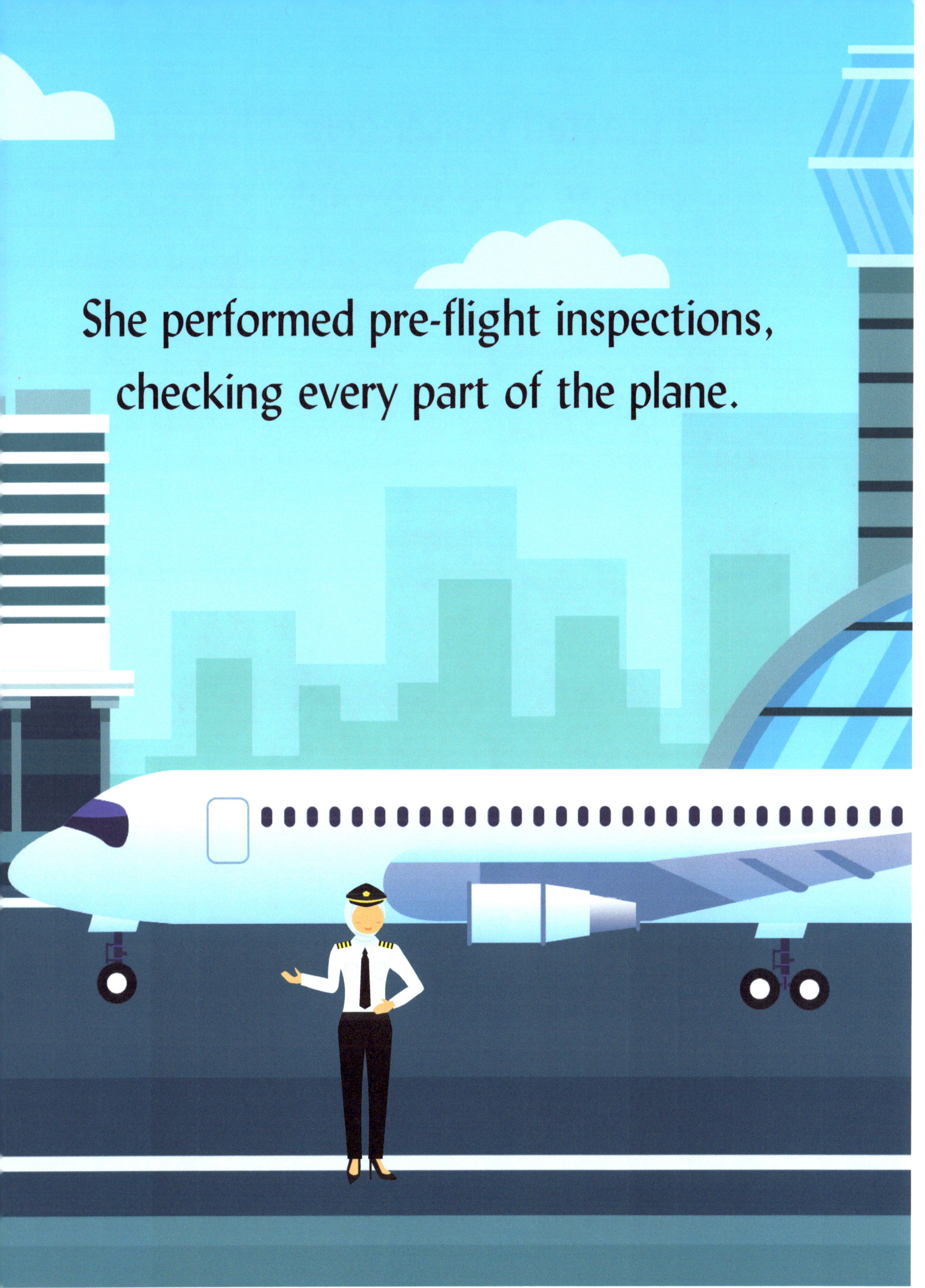

She performed pre-flight inspections,
checking every part of the plane.

She greeted passengers, ensuring everyone was comfortable and safe.

"Welcome aboard!" she announced confidently.

She made announcements before takeoff, explaining the flight details.

In-flight, Parisa made announcements
about altitude and destination.

She reassured passengers, ensuring a smooth and enjoyable flight.

Before landing, Parisa made final announcements, preparing everyone.

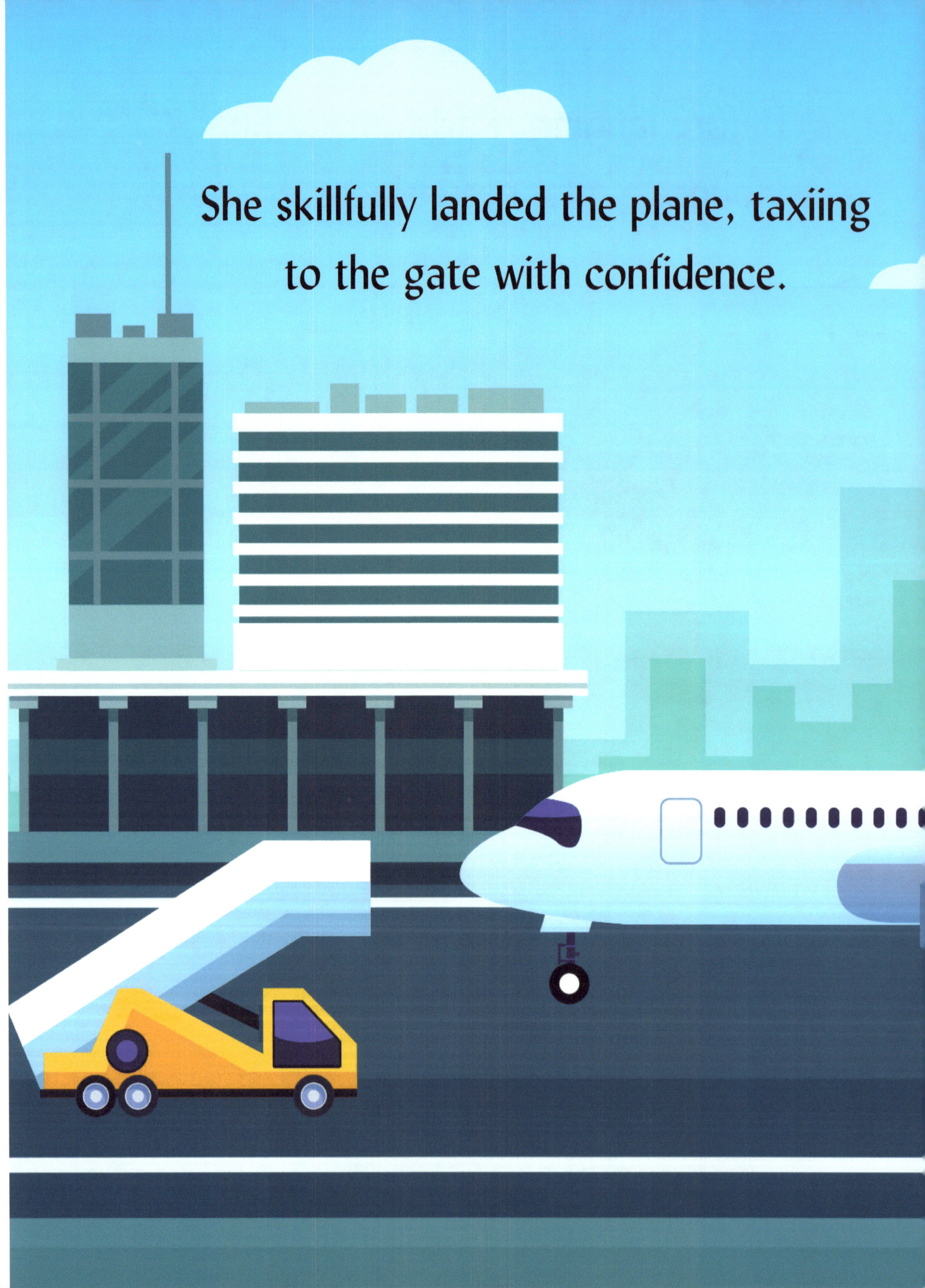

She skillfully landed the plane, taxiing to the gate with confidence.

Parisa said goodbye to passengers, receiving smiles and thank-yous.

Parisa felt a deep
sense of
accomplishment,
having overcome
stereotypes.

Parisa gave speeches, sharing her story and encouraging girls.

She became a mentor, teaching others about flying.

Parisa continued to fly, explore, and inspire everyone she met.

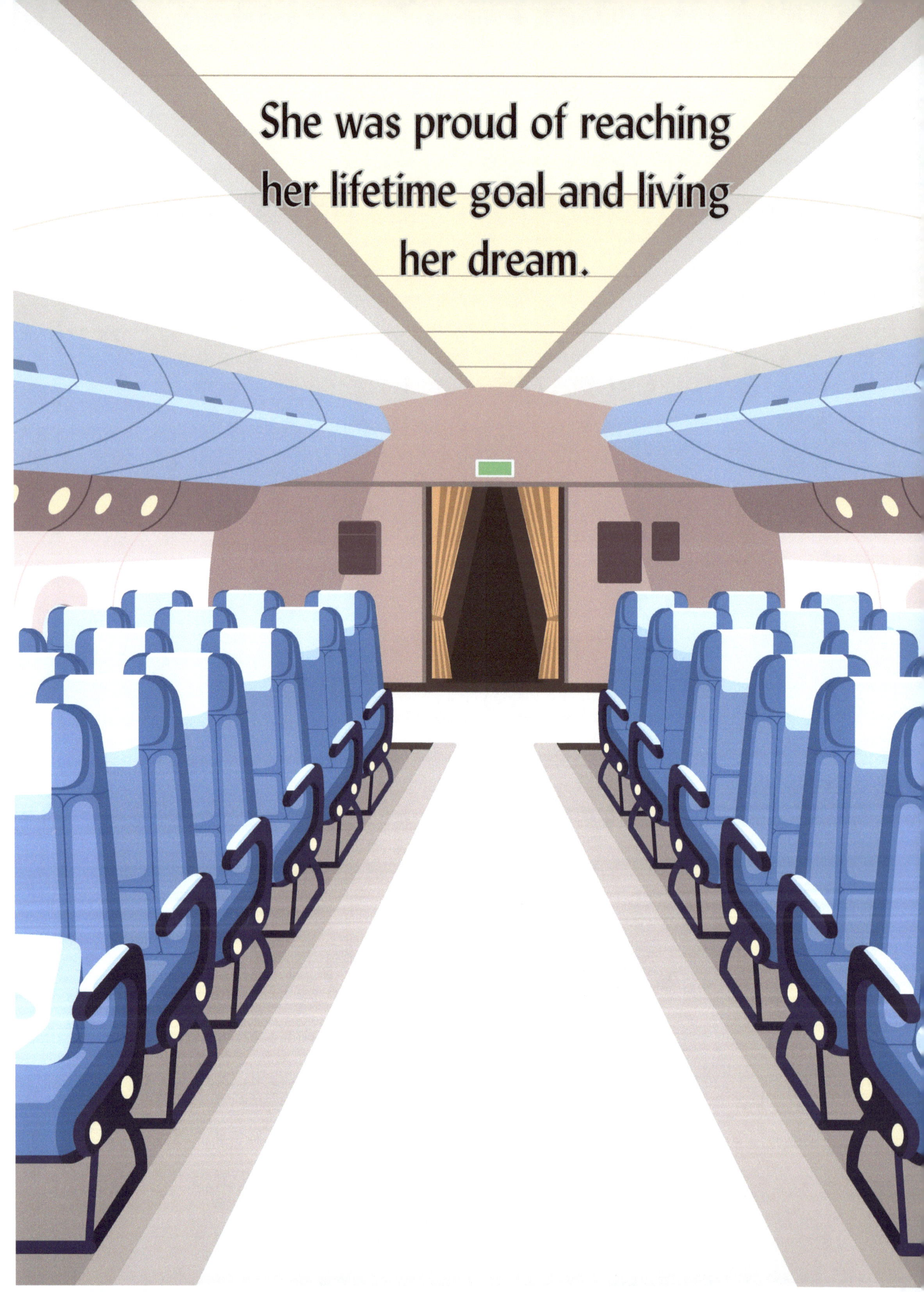
She was proud of reaching
her lifetime goal and living
her dream.

"Girls can be pilots too!"
Parisa proudly declared.

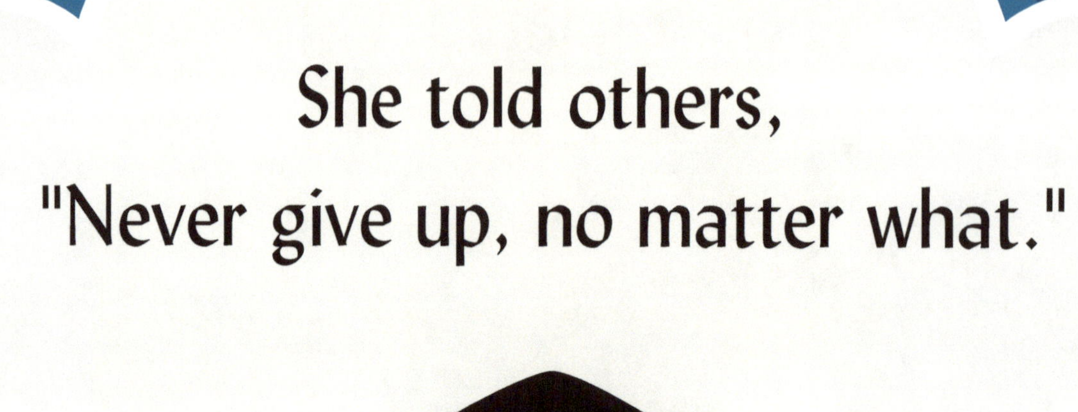

She told others,
"Never give up, no matter what."

The END

Books By Schaaf

www.BookBySchaaf.com

Find us at: